I0493444

Lean Handbook

By Ade Asefeso MCIPS MBA

Copyright 2014 by Ade Asefeso MCIPS MBA
(All rights reserved.)

Second Edition

ISBN-13: 978-1499612875

ISBN-10: 1499612877

Publisher: AA Global Sourcing Ltd
Website: http://www.aaglobalsourcing.com

Table of Contents

Disclaimer

This publication is designed to provide competent and reliable information regarding the subject matter covered. However, it is sold with the understanding that the author and publisher are not engaged in rendering professional advice. The authors and publishers specifically disclaim any liability that is incurred from the use or application of contents of this book.

If you purchased this book without a cover you should be aware that this book may have been stolen property and reported as "unsold and destroyed" to the publisher. In this case neither the author nor the publisher has received any payment for this "stripped book."

Dedication

To my family and friends who seems to have been sent here to teach me something about who I am supposed to be. They have nurtured me, challenged me, and even opposed me.... But at every juncture has taught me!

This book is dedicated to my lovely boys, Thomas, Michael and Karl. Teaching them to manage their finance will give them the lives they deserve. They have taught me more about life, presence, and energy management than anything I have done in my life.

Introduction

The Purpose of this Handbook

This book was written to give a simple explanation of Lean Manufacturing for anyone to understand. It is meant for engineers, purchasing agents, company clerks, newspaper reporters, schoolteachers, or anyone else who wants to find out about Lean.

It is by no means a complete text on Lean, but does include an addendum that will point the way to further Lean knowledge for anyone who is interested.

Lean is a large area of expertise, and no book could possibly cover it all, but it is my hope that you will gain an understanding of Lean principals and be motivated to find out even more about this quiet revolution that is transforming worldwide manufacturing.

What is Lean Manufacturing?

Lean Manufacturing is a manufacturing system and philosophy that was originally developed by Toyota and is now used by many manufacturers throughout the world. At

Toyota the system is referred to as the Toyota Production System. Other manufacturers have adapted the system to meet their own needs and assigned a proprietary name to it. Therefore the term Lean Manufacturing is a more generic term and refers to the general principals and further developments of Lean.

The term Lean is very apt because in Lean Manufacturing the emphasis is to cut out the "fat" or waste in the manufacturing process. Waste is defined as anything that does not add value to the customer. It could also be defined as anything the customer is unwilling to pay for.

For example, if you order a shirt to be custom made, it may take 6 weeks. However the actual time the tailors or seamstresses are working on the shirt is only 5 hours. The rest of the time is taken up by such things as material ordering, waiting between processes and inefficient shipping practices. This extra time does not add value to you, the customer. As Lean Manufacturing principals are applied to the shirt-making process, one would see a reduction in delivery time from 6 to 5 to 4 weeks and even less. The ideal shirt-making operation would be streamlined to give you, the customer, what you want, when you want it at the lowest possible cost within the least amount of time.

Though they may not call it Lean, the "Eyeglasses in About an Hour" companies have applied many Lean principles to their operation. What used to take weeks is now done in about an hour, adding value to the customer. It is no surprise that these operations have opened up all over the country. What was once thought of as impossible speed of delivery is now commonplace. Applying Lean Manufacturing principles gives manufacturers these types of results on a routine basis.

Why did we say "add value to the customer" vs. "add value to the product"?

These are two distinctly different things. For example, a custom made shirt may be made more valuable by adding extra stitching, using top of the line fabric and adding a monogram. All these things add value to the product in terms of quality and the longevity of the product. However, if the customer just wants a basic shirt that fits well and that will last about two years, then these things do not add value to him. He will not be willing to pay a premium to have a more valuable product and the added extras are actually a form of waste.

Another example of this would be UPS Ground vs. Fed Ex overnight. In Indiana one can ship UPS Ground to Michigan and it will arrive the next day over 90% of the time for a cost of about $3 or $4. Fed Ex offers an upgraded product of next day delivery to Michigan 100% of the time. You can even select a 10:30 am delivery time. The price of this service is closer to $10, over twice the cost of the UPS Ground.

Obviously the Fed Ex product has more value. However, in many instances the customer does not require a 100% guarantee and is only willing to pay for a 90% probability of next day delivery. So, unless the customer puts a value on a 100% delivery guarantee, he will be unwilling to pay the extra cost.

Is speed of delivery the main benefit of Lean?

Improved speed of delivery is only one of the benefits of Lean. Lean deals with the reduction or elimination of many types of waste with lowest cost and customer defined quality as driving forces. In Lean technology, identifying and eliminating waste is so important that it even has its own terminology. In Lean, waste is called MUDA, which comes from the Japanese term for waste.

5s

(a.k.a. Visual Workplace, Visual Factory) A workplace organization tool/process that maximizes the cleanliness, organization, and safety of all elements in a working environment.

5S so named for its 5 primary undertakings:
Sort: Remove all unneeded items from the workplace.

Set In Order: Make a place for everything and put everything in its' place.

Shine: Thoroughly clean and inspect everything in the work area (preventative cleaning also applies).

Standardize: Maintain the improvements through discipline and structure.
Sustain: Continue to support 5S efforts through auditing, job descriptions that include maintenance of the system, management support and expectations, etc.

Note: 5S efforts almost always improve workplace safety, operator morale, quality, and throughput. It can also be very impressive to visiting customers and prospective clients.

5 Why's

(a.k.a. "5 Why's and 1 How") A pen and paper tool for discovering the root cause of a problem or issue.

Example:

(1st Why) Why is there oil on the floor?
(Answer after investigation) It is leaking from a hose.

(2nd Why) Why is oil leaking from this hose?
(Answer after investigation) The hose is rubbing on a fan belt.

(3rd Why) Why is it rubbing on the fan belt?
(Answer after investigation) The fan belt housing is very loose.

(4th Why) Why is the fan belt housing so loose?
(Answer after investigation) Some of the bolts that hold it in place are missing or broken off.

(1 How) How do we fix the problem?
(Answer) Replace the hose and fan belt, remove broken bolts on fan belt housing and replace with new ones, torque all bolts to

proper specifications, check bolt torque with regular preventative maintenance.

Note: You probably noticed our example only includes 4 whys. The number of whys is much less important than finding and fixing the root cause of the problem you are having.

6 Sigma

A scientific/data-driven approach for achieving 6 standard deviations between the mean and nearest specifications limit. Six Sigma methods can be applied to all aspects of manufacturing, transactional processes, and virtually any form of work or processing.

Comments: In application we have found a Lean Manufacturing approach to correcting serious problems and realizing significant gains followed by using 6 Sigma methods to "fine tune" and realize further gains to be a very effective strategy.

Many now use the term "Lean Sigma" to reinforce the cooperative nature and capabilities of each improvement tool.

7 Wastes

(a.k.a. "7 Deadly Wastes of Manufacturing", "7 Sins of Manufacturing", etc.) The 7 wastes are activities identified and categorized as non-value adding events or processes that limit profitability in a company.

First identified by Taiichi Ohno of Toyota, the "7 Wastes" are as follows: (simplified)
1. Overproduction: Making more parts than you can sell.

2. Delay: Waiting for processing, parts sitting in storage, etc.

3. Transporting: Parts/Materials: Moving parts to various storage locations, from process to process, etc.

4. Over-Processing: Doing more "work" to a part than is required.
5. Inventory: Committing money and storage space to parts not sold.

6. Motion: Moving parts more than the minimum needed to complete and ship them.

7. Making Defective Parts: Creating parts that cannot be sold "as is" or that must be reworked etc.

Note 1: This is a terrific list and is commonly accepted as all-inclusive. Of course being "Improvers" we add "Innovation" as Number 8 which includes failing to tap into the human potential and creativity of your workforce. We contend that this is perhaps among the greatest failures and "wastes" in manufacturing today.

Note 2: Another waste, "Re-prioritization" (Number 9 if you will,) has also become more accepted in the Lean community. It is the practice of incurring waste by doing things like changing from one project or run of materials etc. before its "natural" and/or scheduled conclusion. This may cause increased losses due to setups and customer delivery delays etc. This is the commonly known practice of someone in authority declaring a job "HOT" and prioritizing it to the detriment of other jobs / customer's needs.

Activity Based Costing

Activity Based Costing (ABC) is a costing system that identifies the various activities performed in a firm and uses multiple cost drivers (non-volume as well as the volume based cost drivers) to assign overhead costs (or indirect costs) to products. ABC Costing considers the impact and relationship of cost drivers with activities performed.

Example: Every "widget" you produce was sitting in a building that you are paying for. Therefore every "widget" has cost added to it by virtue of it being in your plant. Consider also the electricity, water, air conditioning, etc. that have an impact on every product you produce.

Abc Inventory

ABC Inventory is a methodology for determining inventory levels based on value, space consumption, and turns.

Example: Generally the following "rules" apply:

"A" type inventory is very expensive (keep as little on hand as is reasonable so you don't tie up too much cash in inventory.)

"B" type inventory is only moderately or middle of the road expensive (Minimize this inventory to free up cash also, but if you have a little extra it won't break the bank.)

"C" type inventory is fairly inexpensive (If it consumes little space and costs very little don't lose any sleep over it. That said, you should keep this inventory to a reasonable minimum as well.

Note: There is much more to explain on this topic, but this should get you started when engaging in an inventory reduction process.

Andon

A "Visual Control" device that indicates the "Status" of a machine, line, or process. Frequently audible alarms or warning messages accompany ANDON status lights as a secondary method of communicating a problem has arisen.

ANDONS are typically colour-coded with these generic colours:

Green (Normal Operations)

Yellow (It is time for a changeover or planned maintenance)

Red (A problem has occurred, the machine or line is "DOWN," and "Urgent attention is needed.

Comments: As Lean practitioners we have seen ANDON lights and warning sounds being very effective in certain settings and within a disciplined Lean culture. Conversely, we have seen them very much ignored and therefore disconnected due to their annoying qualities and lack of discipline.

ANDON's can be very effective in highly automated processes to alert support personnel of problems who must attend to several automated processes at a time or are not located in close proximity to the machines they oversee.

Autonomation

Stopping a machine automatically or without intervention when a defective part has been created.

Comments: Some forms of Autonomation do include human intervention to detect defective parts but the ideal is to have a machine detect a defective part and then correct the problem on its own.

Autonomation devices can be very complex involving sensing equipment, lasers, scales, etc. or it can be as simple as parts not being able to pass through a dimensional gauge. This method typically causes a backing-up of the system which at some point triggers a shut-down switch or alarm to gain operator attention to the problem.

Available to Promise

Software tools that provide customers and customer service representatives access to product order delivery dates in real-time (while on the phone placing orders or shortly after the order has been taken). This utility can often interface with inventory replenishment, forecasting, and scheduling/planning.

Balanced Production

When a manufacturing system/entity produces "exactly" (+ or -) what their customers demand it is said to be "in balance"

Note: Takt Time is the measurement most often used to determine if a manufacturing plant is "balanced."

If a product's Takt Time is "1 part every 30 seconds" and the manufacturer can only produce "1 part every 40 seconds" then there will be a shortfall and the plant is not "in balance" with its customers

Likewise, if a plant produces "1 part every 15 seconds" they are overproducing (see 7 wastes), and are not "in balance" with their customers.

Batch Manufacturing

(a.k.a. "Batch Processing") Producing lots or quantities of a product in order to achieve maximum "Economic Order Quantities" (EOQ).

Comments: Although some products must be batched to maximize use of equipment with long cycle times, often batching is wrongly assumed to be more economical than single piece production for various reasons.

Often when large "batches" are the preferred operating mode it is due to excessively long or difficult changeover practices. Improving changeover techniques through SMED implementation will generally minimizes lot or "batch" sizes, reduce finished goods inventory on-hand, allow for increased varieties of products that can be made more quickly, and ultimately lead to greater customer responsiveness.

Benchmarking

A comparison tool used to determine the level of process, product, or other successes your company is experiencing when compared to similar companies with similar products or processes; typically competitors.

Methods include tracking metrics like On-time Delivery, Defective Parts Per Million produced, wages paid, market share growth and projections, etc.

Note: Most successful companies use benchmarking to identify strengths and weakness as compared to competitors and make needed adjustments.

Bottleneck

The slowest operation (choke point) in a manufacturing process.

Do not confuse this with a company's "Constraint" taken from TOC (Theory of Constraints), which is the slowest operation in an entire manufacturing system that, if remedied, would increase overall company throughput.

Example: In a work cell containing 5 dissimilar machines, the 3rd machine in the cell takes twice as long to cycle as the other machines. No products will leave this cell until they have gone through the slowest process or "bottleneck" (machine number 3). This is the "bottleneck" operation in this cell.

Bump Back

Helping the person(s) before or after another person in a manufacturing cell or system.

Example: Let's say my operation is a little faster than that of the person before me who supplies me with work. I can in some cases finish part of their process so that I will continue to have parts to work on.

If too much Bump-Back work is happening it may be that you should re-evaluate the tasks undertaken at each work station in the cell.

Capability

The maximum achievable results that can be attained in a manufacturing system based on limitations imposed.

Example: McDonald's could not build a complete aircraft carrier in its' kitchen, but it could create a fine "Big Mac tm."

Size, weight, complexity of parts, environmental regulations, and processes (to name a few) all figure in to determining the capability of a manufacturing system.

Note: Some definitions propose an opposing notion that capability is merely what is possible based on limitations. We prefer the more positive definition sited above.

Capacity

The maximum amount a process, machine, or system can produce.

Comments: If a machine is running "at capacity" it is going as fast as it can go and producing as much as it can produce.

If a machine is running "below capacity" it is able to do more than it is currently doing.

It is sometimes not necessary or desirable to run machines "at capacity." Most cars will exceed 100 miles per hour but that excess capacity is typically not needed or advisable.

Cause and Effect Diagram

A problem-solving tool that graphically illustrates the relationship(s) between various process elements which prepares problem solvers to assess the impact of variation from standard.

Example: If "widget" production is charted on 3 similar machines and two machines produce equal amounts of "widgets" per hour while one machine produces 20% fewer parts per hour (as per drawn or charted data) then a variable exists that is "causing" the poorer performance of the third machine.

Since the best "widget" producing machines run on electricity and regulated air pressure these variables could be having a negative impact on production. Diagramming each element will show (perhaps) that machine number 3 was running at 80 p.s.i. instead of 120 p.s.i. like the other two machines.

Cellular Manufacturing

(a.k.a. U-Shaped Cells, Work Cells) Generally a horseshoe or U-Shaped work area layout that enables workers to easily move from one process to another in close proximity and pass parts between workers with little effort. "Cells" typically focus on the production of specific models in "part families" but can be adjusted to many different products as needed.

Comments: Work Cells do not need to be in a U-shaped configuration though this is often common due to maximizing product throughput with minimal use of space. We have created Work Cells in many different configurations that resemble letters like T, W, X, V, etc.; it is also common to create polygons, circles, rectangles, etc.

The ultimate layout of the cell is determined by the needs of the product. The goal in laying out a new Work Cell is to pass a part through every needed process with the minimal amount of wasted motion and distance. On the next level the layout of the Work Cell is determined by the manual and machine cycle times and "Takt Time" in order to determine Cell staffing.

Other issues when creating cells include redundancy of equipment, size of equipment needed, cure times, and Cell mobility/flexibility to accommodate multiple products.

When Work Cells are laid out most efficiently they can usually produce parts with a staff of 1 person moving from station to station (Load-Load), or fully staffed with a worker at each station. Product demand helps determine staffing.

Example: (Note: Many other configurations can work as well.) cells

Change Agent

Person(s) who lead a company from the traditional manufacturing practices and philosophies to becoming a Lean organization.

Comments: As Lean consultants we are Change Agents but the power to change for the better should be grown and nurtured within each company.

Nothing helps a company change and improve like a committed senior management.

Changeovers

Switching from producing one part/product to another is generally known as a changeover.

Comments: This switching or Changeover process may involve removing and replacing dies from machine beds, removing and replacing unused materials such as changing from corn to wheat in a food hopper, black plastic to white plastic in an injection moulding bin, etc.

In Lean Manufacturing terms changeovers are best accomplished through S.M.E.D. "Single Minute Exchange of Die." This strives to complete a changeover in less than 10 minutes.

Co-location

Physically locating personnel and product lines in a single area thereby enabling rapid and constant communication among the key personal responsible for those products.

Comments: Many companies now co-locate sales, customer service, engineering, administrative, production, and other functions in an attempt to create a fairly independent and full-service department that focuses on a single product or product family.

There are pros and cons to this approach as many redundant roles are common. The up-side is that there is an expertise and almost "omniscient" awareness of customer needs, and production status.

Concurrent Engineering

The reorganization of product design, development, production planning and procurement processes to take place to the extent possible in parallel (more or less at the same time), utilizing multi-disciplinary project teams, electronic information management, and improved communications.

Input is gathered and assimilated from all concerned parties, including manufacturing, sales, procurement, customers, and etc. from project conception throughout development.

Comments: No manufacturing plant is better off engineering products in a vacuum. This approach challenges earlier out-dated thinking that the engineers will hand-over new products when they have designed them. With concurrent Engineering all (most in reality), of the stakeholders have a say in the design of products.

We have often encountered products that were so difficult to manufacture because engineers were unaware of certain machine idiosyncrasies or limitations, or human effort required to manufacture the products.

Constraint

Taken from (TOC) "Theory of Constraints" A constraint is anything that limits a system from achieving higher performance relative to its' goal.

Comments: In practical application a "Company's Constraint" is the biggest limiting factor that reduces the amount of throughput the company can achieve. This may mean a machine or process that is the slowest operation (bar none). A company can have many bottlenecks, but in order to be the Constraint of the company it must be the "Alpha Bottleneck" that affects the throughput of the company as a whole.

Some companies have more than one Constraint. Although one may be slightly larger than another, working to "break" 2 or 3 constraints of approximately the same size or limiting nature simultaneously is of worthwhile pursuit.

Continuous Improvement

The ongoing process/philosophy of doing things better, faster, and cheaper.

Comments: A Lean Manufacturing system or organization will usually effect many large-scale and far-reaching changes while implementing Lean as a company directive. After the big "bang for the buck" Lean tools have been implemented there can be a tendency toward complacency. A structured Continuous Improvement process enables an organization to refine and enhance the benefits they now enjoy as a Lean company through usually small and incremental changes within the system.

Example: Stamping press number 8 typically produces 27 parts per minute (ppm) but "Takt Time" tells us we now need 30 ppm. The press is already running "at capacity" so a decision must be made to purchase a similar press or somehow get 3 more ppm out of press number 8.

Using a Continuous Improvement process a Kaizen Team would carefully examine the possibility of getting more production out of the machine before buying another one.

Perhaps replacing worn belts, hydraulic pumps, regulators, shortening the "stroke" of the machine, or any number of other fixes would improve the machine enough to avoid buying a new one to meet current demand.

Continuous Flow

Moving products through a production system without separating them into lots.

Comments: Basically, once you begin producing a product you keep it moving through the value stream without placing it into a holding area for later processing. This helps avoid "batching" and increasing inventory levels.

In the ideal production system we attempt to achieve "1-piece flow" in which each product is passed or moved along in the production process independently until it is completed and ready to be shipped to a waiting customer. There may be 100 pieces in a shipping container, but each piece was processed individually throughout the value stream.

If a product needs a process like anodizing for example, it may flow continuously until a certain point at which time this process must take place and then be "batched" for anodizing (perhaps mixed with other products). It can later be individually processed until its completion. This would not be purely a "continuous flow" process but practical reality.

Creative Problem Solving

Methods that combine defining of problems, identification of patterns, generation of new ideas, and action planning to resolve problems with unique and innovative solutions.

Example: One "Brainstorming" exercise we use to "open" closed minds is to ask a Kaizen team to list ways they might retrieve a basketball from a rooftop.

Upon completion of this exercise we generally have a list of more than 100 very original ways to remove the ball from the roof. Although many of the methods would be extreme and not practical to employ, they serve as springboards to other ideas that may be highly creative and useful.

Getting ball off roof: Ladder, rake, helicopter, bb gun, slingshot, dynamite, trained pigeon, monkey, etc. This is a fun exercise that really helps people change the way they look at problem solving.

Current State or "As Is" Map

Taken from Value Stream Mapping, (VSM) the "Current State Map" shows the value stream or process map as it is operating right now.

Comments: Very often the "Current State Map" will illustrate significant differences between how things are in reality and the documented processes and procedures.

The "Current State Map" is used as a springboard for creating an "Ideal State Map" which (with significant improvements) removes wasteful practices from the value stream.

Cycle Time

The time it takes to do one repetition of any particular task typically measured from "Start to Start" the starting point of one product's processing in a specified machine or operation until the start of another similar product's processing in the same machine or process. Cycle time is commonly categorized into:

1) Manual Cycle Time: The time loading, unloading, flipping/turning parts, adding components to parts while still in the same machine/process etc.

2) Machine Cycle Time: The processing time of the machine working on a part.

3) Auto Cycle Time: The time a machine runs un-aided (automatically) without manual intervention.

4) Overall Cycle Time: The complete time it takes to produce a single unit. This term is generally used when speaking of a single machine or process.

5) Total Cycle Time: This includes all machines, processes, and classes of cycle time through which a product must pass to become a finished product. This is not Lead Time, but it does help in determining it.

Note: In most cases it doesn't matter very much which form of cycle time is greatest. What does matter is that your "Total Cycle Time" is less than your "Takt Time."

Demand Management

(a.k.a. Demand Forecasting) Prediction of the levels of weekly or monthly product activity over a specified time (generally about two years).

Comments: MRP II systems seem to be at least in part responsible for encouraging this practice.

Distribution Management

A tool for deciding upon and producing the optimal quantities of products needed from each plant to supply distribution warehouses/centres with sufficient products to meet customer demand with minimal costs and risks incurred.

Comments: Since multiple plants often collaborate to supply customers with products across a large geographic area a comprehensive distribution management system is very helpful in maintaining minimal product quantities without risking out-of-stock problems that ultimately hurt customers and company.

Overstocking warehouses would be one of the "7 Wastes" causing a company to lose money invested in inventory, risk obsolescence, and need larger warehouses, etc.

Empowerment

Giving employees more responsibility, authority, and accountability for effecting the daily processes and improvements within their job environment.

Comments: "Empowered Teams" or "Self-Directed Work Teams "are an advanced framework for running a work area or department. Many of the best companies invest in the Empowered Teams strategy as a means for creating self-regulating entities that require little supervision and support.

If you consider the most productive managers are the best delegators then you begin to appreciate in a small way the power behind "Empowered" or "Self-Directed Work Teams."

Enterprise Resources Planning

Taking the needs of an entire organization into account "ERP" Enterprise Resources Planning is essentially an extension of "MRP" "Manufacturing Resources Planning" which attempts to ascertain needs and abilities of a company system.

Comments: Both ERP and MRP systems have been getting a lot of attention over the last several years and can have particular value when it comes to very large organizations with thousands of sku's.

Very often we find many "work-around's" to these systems which greatly compromises their usefulness and data. As software and understanding of systems improves these tools should become more useful.

Error and Mistake-Proofing

(a.k.a. Poka-Yoke (Japanese) Lean tool for making products correctly the first time.

Comments: When thoroughly implemented Error and Mistake-Proofing create improvements on many different levels. Even the products themselves may be redesigned to minimize errors in their manufacture.

Tooling and processes are often reworked to produce error-free parts or at minimum catch errors before they become significant defects that require rework or become scrap.

Example: One common and popular example of Mistake-Proofing is the design of the VHS video tape player. A videotape will only fully enter a VCR and play if it is placed correctly into opening.

External Setup

Steps and procedures that can be performed while a machine is still operating that facilitate the SMED "Single Minute Exchange of Die" process.

Comments: The most powerful technique used in many SMED applications is converting all "Internal Setup" (procedures that can only be completed while a machine is not operating) to "External Setup" procedures. Typically this one step will reduce setup/changeover times by + or − 50%!

Failure Modes and Effects Analysis

A systematic/structured approach for determining the seriousness of potential failures and for identifying the sources of each potential failure.

The goal of "FMEA" failure modes and effects analysis is to identify potential failures and implement corrective actions to prevent failures from occurring. "PFMEA" focuses on identifying and remediating process failures.

Comments: Essentially all parts and or processes will eventually fail (at least occasionally). The FMEA process will help you minimize how serious and common failures are and the impact they have. Attention to FMEA during development phases of products or processes can pay huge dividends.

Using FMEA tools after products or processes have been developed is probably more common than employing them during development in general. Generally we find FMEA efforts employed to "fix" critical issues with a part or process problem after it has become very serious. It tends to be a "reactive" rather than "proactive" endeavour in most companies we have experience with.

First In First Out

A system for keeping track of the order in which information or materials are to be processed. The goal of First In First Out "FIFO" is to prevent earlier orders from being delayed in favour of newer orders which would result in increased lead time and unhappy customers regarding the earlier orders.

Note: FIFO can usually be implemented in a very straightforward fashion and makes a good deal of sense on an intuitive and practical level. Where FIFO falls short is the shortcomings and emotional decisions made by humans to circumvent the system. Customers that are considered more "important" than others test the will and commitment of even the most stalwart FIFO advocates.

Fishbone Diagram

A problem-solving tool that uses a graphic description of the various process elements to analyze potential sources of variation, or problems. The Diagram itself resembles (somewhat) the skeleton of a fish.

Comments: Fishbone Diagrams help people begin to visualize the relationships between the various aspects of simple or complex problems. They are particularly helpful to people who prefer to solve problems using visual and written information.

Even newly formed teams can use Fishbone Diagrams to help resolve unfamiliar problems.

Flexible Automation

Highly mechanized (often robotic) method for switching from one product type or style to another product type or style. Key in FA is automatic changeovers of dies, materials such as adhesives, and usually small components.

Comments: These systems can be especially useful when working with very small parts that are produced in very high volume and are difficult for human hands and tools to manipulate.

Flexible Manufacturing System

Flexible Manufacturing System (FMS) is a manufacturing process/system designed so that production areas (such as work cells or lines) can be changed and rebalanced often to adjust labour and materials to better meet and match demand.

Example: In a manufacturing cell we used reversible supply racks and alternate hanging tools that could be immediately employed when the cell would convert from one product line (Brand) to another.

Flow Chart

A visual description of the steps in a process or system.

Comments: Simple Flow Charts help in illustrating every step in a process in a concrete way so they can then be analyzed for improvement opportunities and division of labour etc.

Gemba

A Japanese term that means "Real Place" or "Where the action takes place." In Lean we speak of GEMBA as being the place where "Value" is added to a product. See "Value Adding"

Comments: In the most practical sense Lean attempts to make everything in a factory "GEMBA" or a value adding process or location.

The antonym of GEMBA is MUDA or "Waste" which Lean practitioners do all in their power to eliminate.

Goal

Measurable statement of specific intent bounded by a specific period of time.

Comments: S.M.A.R.T. Goals are:
Specific: We will change by "x" amount.

Measurable: We are now at "x" amount and will be at "x" amount after improvements.

Attainable: These are reachable results even though they may require some "stretch" to achieve.

Relevant: The desired results are pertinent to the people and area working on them well within their range of things they are allowed to change.

Timely: Specific dates are important. We will change "x" by 9/22/2213.
Example: The Metal Fab dept. will reduce scrap on the 600 ton press by 10% from 100 pieces per day to 90 pieces per day by 8/01/25.

Group Technology

(A.k.a. GT, Part Families) Group Technology (GT) separates parts into "Families" or groups that have similar needs with respect to manufacturing processes. Parts may be "grouped" by size weight, colour, flavour, chemistry, treatments/special processing needed, etc.

Comments: Creating "Part Families" or "Groups" can result in lower inventories, reduced consumption of process resources, and many other benefits.

On an intuitive level and for the purpose of identifying and exposing your "Value Stream" grouping parts into "families" can help to identify further improvement opportunities.

Ideal State Map

(a.k.a. "Future State" or "Should Be" Map) A future-looking version of a process map (VSM) "Value Stream Mapping" depicting how a process will work after improvements are implemented.

Comments: Creating a Future State Map is a great exercise for helping your improvement teams catch the vision of where you are going in your Lean process. This map can be created to some degree immediately following the creation of your "Current State Map" or after significant improvements have been made.

We recommend creating an Ideal State Map very early in your VSM process to help set the focus for your improvement efforts.

Innovation

Creating something new i.e., an idea, device or processing method; Invention.

Comments: Identified by Throughput Solutions as the "8th Waste" in "Ohno's 7 Wastes of Manufacturing," we recognize that the potential for innovation available in every workforce is largely not realized.

We further assert that "Un-tapped Human Potential" to include innovation and inventiveness in all their forms, represents the single greatest losses or "wastes" experienced in manufacturing today.

Internal Customers

In a manufacturing environment "Internal Customers" are the people, machines, or processes being supplied with the products or parts made in preceding work area(s).

Comments: Although both areas (the supplying and receiving areas) work for the same company, it is a good practice for everyone and every department to treat those they supply to as if they were prized customers. This attention to courtesy, delivery performance, and special needs within the Internal Customer area will yield a positive interaction, improve communications, and increase throughput.

Very often we find Internal Supplier areas not communicating with Internal Customers areas or perhaps, even worse competing with each other. Building the "Customer/Supplier" relationship is part of changing to a "Lean Culture" as an organization.

Internal Setup

Taken from (SMED): These are setup procedures that can only be effected when a machine is in a "Zero Mechanical State."

Comments: The goal of SMED is to change dies or other components/processes in under 10 minutes. "Internal" setup elements that require machines to be completely inoperable are one of the greatest sources of waste during a setup/changeover process. Therefore, much time and attention is dedicated to discovering how machines can continue running during most or all of the changeover process.

If a SMED Kaizen Team can make "Internal" setup procedures "External" they will generally reduce setup/changeover times by at least 50%.

Internal Suppliers

Are the people, machines, or processes delivering or supplying products or parts they have made to the next (in sequence) work area(s).

Comments: Internal Suppliers have an opportunity to satisfy an "Internal Customer" by delivering quality products, on time, every time, where their Internal Customers want them, how they want them, etc.

Essentially, everyone and every department is someone's customer and someone's supplier. Departments may have many different Internal Suppliers and Internal Customers. Whether an individual or a department has only one or many customers/suppliers they should always treat them as if they were "prized customers" or "valued suppliers."
This is a critical issue to effecting a Lean Manufacturing Culture Change.

Inventory

The money and materials invested in by a company in order to create products for sale.

Comments: In truth there are few areas that can yield more outstanding initial cost savings than the reduction of inventory in many, if not most companies. Inventory must be viewed as "MONEY" and treated accordingly.

The most common types of Inventory are:
Raw Materials: Un-processed components waiting for work to be done on them. This is the least expensive form of inventory especially if suppliers will wait for payment until you begin using these materials.

Work in Process (W.I.P.): Materials that have had some work done to them but are not yet finished. This is the second most expensive form of inventory as "value" has been added to the materials.

Finished Goods: This is the most expensive type of inventory as the materials have already travelled through the value stream and are now complete. Although most companies

carry some Finished Goods Inventory it can
be a serious waste and burden on cash-flow.

Note: Some consider staff members to be a
form of inventory as well as machines,
buildings, electricity, innovation, and etc.

Inventory Turns

The number of times you can "Turn" (use and replace) your inventory/money over in a year.

Comments: This is a bit of a tough concept for many people so we will use a very basic explanation.

If your company holds $1000 worth of inventory every month and consumes $1000 worth of inventory every month that would equal "12 Inventory Turns per year."

The "real world" is not as "clean" as the example above, and it can be challenging to "know" how many times each year you "turn" your inventory.

Some companies will speak of inventory turns specific to individual parts or materials, i.e., "We turn our raw widget parts every week, or "We have 24 turns a year on our coiled steel."

The real message behind Inventory Turns is to keep enough inventory on-hand to satisfy your customers but not so much that it ends-up collecting dust and costing you money in the form of lost interest, damage, obsolescence, storage space, moving it around, etc.

Just-in-Time

Just-in-Time (JIT) is a Lean Manufacturing process for synchronizing materials, operators, and equipment such that all materials and people are where they need to be, when they need to be there, and in the state they need to be there in.

Comments: JIT is ultimately focused on reducing or eliminating every form of waste in the manufacturing process. Many Lean Manufacturing tools help to make achieving a Just-in-Time system possible.

Example: It doesn't matter much if materials arrive at a machine for processing when the machine is "down" due to poor maintenance. A TPM "Total Productive Maintenance" program could remedy this situation.

Likewise, if it takes several hours to change-out dies materials could spend substantially more time waiting for processing than actually being processed. SMED efforts are warranted to enable quick changeovers and allow JIT methods to be effectively employed.

Kaizen Implementation Team

(a.k.a. "Kaizen Team(s)" "Improvement Team(s)") Team(s) that implements the Lean Manufacturing tools needed to effect improvements.

Comments: Many companies use a single "Kaizen Team" to effect the changes brought about by Lean Manufacturing. We do not recommend this approach as it limits the input and engagement of the workforce in general.

We recommend multiple Kaizen Teams engaging in the improvement process through the implementation and refinement of Lean Manufacturing tools and undertakings. It becomes the "2 heads are better than one" approach and motivates employees plant-wide to become involved in the evolution and improvement of the company.

Kan-Ban

A Japanese term meaning "visual record" or "card." In Lean Manufacturing speak Kan-Ban has come to mean "Signal."

Comments: So what is Kan-Ban signalling? Kan-Ban "signals" are basically just telling workers that there is more work to be done. In other words, the presence of a "Kan-Ban Card" or an empty "Kan-Ban Location" is a "signal" to do the work described on the card (make the parts) or fill the empty Kan-Ban location with parts which means you have to make them to put them there.

There are many ways to use and implement Kan-Bans like empty totes, pallets, cartons, flashing lights, electronic messages, etc. You can even park a semi truck at a certain dock and that could be your signal to produce parts that will be shipped via this truck. There is no limit to the creativity you can have with Kan-Ban signals. One key is to make them work in your specific situation and environment.

Perhaps the most important rule of Kan-Ban is to "Obey Kan-Ban." In other words do not go around the system or it will fail. Failing to keep the rules of Kan-Ban will result in higher inventories, greater risk for errors/defects, and other associated problems.

Now that we have emphasized keeping the rules of Kan-Ban we must discuss a few reasonable exceptions. Breaking Kan-Ban limits to production should occur if a machine has broken but will be able to catch up as soon as it is repaired. Yes, you will be building inventories, but this machines cycles faster than the feeding machine(s) and will be able to process the "TEMPORARY" glut of WIP "Work in Process" parts.

One more exception might be breaking Kan-Ban to create parts for a customer or sister company that suddenly and desperately needs parts that are only finished to a certain degree. You may find yourself off-loading a machine or process to feed temporary work cells to meet this unexpected and "temporary" demand.

Generally speaking you'll want to stick with Kan-Ban and follow its' basic rules. It works better that way.

Last in First Out

Last In First Out (L.I.F.O.) is the opposite of "F.I.F.O." (First In First Out). With LIFO earlier orders are delayed in favour of newer orders which results in increased lead-time and unhappy customers regarding the earlier orders.

Comments: Both LIFO and FIFO can also be a reference to the order in which stock is consumed. Generally speaking companies should use their oldest stock before using the newest stock. This becomes very important with perishable goods and goods with limited shelf-life.

As consultants we have seen dust more than 1/4th of an inch thick on stock that should have been consumed in order of purchase years earlier. It is difficult to decide in many cases whether this stock is still good to use, has become obsolete in some way, has some latent defect, and etc.

Many advanced material handling systems, stacking systems, and simple Kan-Ban methods can keep your inventory stocked in FIFO order to avoid the many pitfalls of LIFO failings.

All that said, there are times when LIFO measures seem essential. If a customer who represents the majority of your sales requests something immediately it is very difficult to tell them they must wait their turn.

Lead-Time

The time required from receipt of order until products are shipped to a customer.

Notes: Sometimes the single biggest difference between competing companies is the amount of Lead-Time they will commit to. If company "A" promises they will have your products delivered to your door in 6 weeks and company "B" promises a 1 week delivery which company will you likely choose?

Lean Manufacturing has many tools that ultimately reduce Lead-Time and win market share.

Oddly enough Inventory in a manufacturing system has the limiting effect of increasing Lead-Time. Chew on that one for awhile.

Lean Enterprise

(a.k.a. Lean Manufacturing) An organization that is engaged in the endless pursuit of waste elimination in all of its' activities.

Comments: Lean Enterprise focuses on all aspects of a company's system. Whereas Lean Manufacturing tends to focus on production activities, Lean Enterprises are diligently working to reduce waste in all of its many forms in every department and activity the organization engages in.

Lean Enterprises reduce or eliminate paperwork, improve supply chain agreements, enhance hiring and training processes, provide employee development opportunities, and many other such activities.

Lean Manufacturing

(a.k.a. Lean Production) A manufacturing/production system best characterized as relentlessly eliminating waste from all of its' activities and operations. Lean strives to produce products:

On-Time
Using as few resources as possible
Better than competitors. Faster and cheaper than competitors.

Comments: Lean Manufacturing is the "umbrella" under which many manufacturing improvement tools are housed. Some examples include:

SMED: Single Minute Exchange of DIE.

TPM: Total Productive Maintenance.

5S: Visual Workplace or Visual Factory.

Kan-Ban: Work Signalling System.

2-Bin: Materials Replenishment system

Error and Mistake-Proofing: A perfect process tool.

Level-Loading (Heijunka): For producing mixed quantities and styles of products. (And the list goes on...)

Lean Manufacturing is now present throughout the world and has become a global standard or set of practices which virtually all companies must adopt in order to be competitive in a global economy.

Beyond the "need" to compete globally Lean empowers and motivates employees to engage in the betterment of their respective companies. It is also good fun!

Level Loading and Mixed Level Loading

(a.k.a. Heijunka, Balancing) A Technique used to balance production throughput according to the needs of customers (Demand).

Comments: Level-Loading is loading your production system according to the exact needs (+ or -) of your customers. Ideally it is based on the consumption of products customers are "pulling" from your system.

Mixed-Level-Loading supports the same concept as Level-Loading which is to supply your customers with exactly what they need when they need it. However, "mixing" includes producing perhaps many different models of products in correct quantities and ratios to satisfy customer demand for a variety of products with shorter than average lead-times.

Level and Mixed-Level Loading are advanced Lean methods and require a good deal of Lean implementation before they can be very successfully applied in "real world" plants. You must have the ability to switch from one product to another very quickly (usually automatically) to make this system work.

Often you will need to modify tooling to accept a variety of parts so that no changeover process is required at all.

Example: One particular client of ours is an automotive OEM plant. They are so good at Mixed-Level-Loading that on one small conveyor you will often see 2 or 3 Toyota parts followed by 1 or 2 GM parts, followed by 4 or 5 Nissan parts, followed by 2 Toyota parts, followed by 6 or 8 Ford parts, followed by…

You get the point! Finding the right "mix" to satisfy each customer "real-time" is much easier than being able to produce that mix. Putting all the best Lean tools in place will enable you to eventually take your production to this pinnacle level of performance.

Manufacturability

The extent to which a product can be efficiently manufactured with maximum reliability.

Comments: Many products are very difficult to produce and are very often not designed to be mass produced. Sadly, only after a good number of failures and a host of frustrated employees have complained do many product designers finally consider easier, faster, and more reliable ways of manufacturing parts.

We urge product designers to work closely with engineering, production, tooling, and even operators when developing products that must later be produced in the thousands or millions. A coordinated effort can make an enormous difference to ultimate successful production.

Manufacturing

The practice of planning, designing, and managing people and machinery to produce useable products.

Manufacturing is the production of goods for use or sale using labour and machines, tools, chemical and biological processing, or formulation.

The term may refer to a range of human activity, from handicraft to high tech, but is most commonly applied to industrial production, in which raw materials are transformed into finished goods on a large scale. Such finished goods may be used for manufacturing other, more complex products, such as aircraft, household appliances or automobiles, or sold to wholesalers, who in turn sell them to retailers, who then sell them to end users; the "consumers".

Manufacturing Execution System

Manufacturing Execution System (MES)
Is a networked computing system used to automate production control and process automation through intercommunication between production scheduling, work scheduling and production throughput to bridge gaps that might appear between these functions.

Manufacturing Resources Planning

Manufacturing Resources Planning (MRP II) is a computerized method for planning the use of a company's resources, such as scheduling raw materials, suppliers/vendors, production equipment and processes.

Comments: Many MRPII systems include distribution management, certain Human Resources Functions, various customizable business critical functions, and toll-gating features etc.

To be blunt as Lean practitioners we tend to employ "Occam's Razor" which paraphrased states that the simplest answer is usually the best. There is a great deal of complexity in these systems and many times their output is ignored or worked-around.

Look for improved planning software that takes Lean principles into account in the near future. Many good people a fair amount brighter than the rest of us are working hard to create truly incredible new systems.

Manufacturing Test/Verify

The process for assuring that products have been produced and function as designed.

Comments: Depending on many different variables certain specifications and measurements are taken to "guarantee" manufactured products work as they are designed. Many companies spend exhaustive amounts of time checking and rechecking their work and documenting ad-infinitum. This is especially true in companies where potentially dangerous or "high-risk" products are made. Companies making Nuclear Reactor components must test, verify, and document even the very smallest details to satisfy themselves that their parts will work as designed and equally importantly satisfy the government that they have proven out their process and products with approved procedures to specifications.

Like any "good thing" we have seen test and verify processes significantly impact companies in very negative ways. Some companies have engaged in testing processes that unnecessarily consumed days of what could have been production time and many hours of labour while they consistently yield no measurable gains resulting from all of the extra effort.

Leaner and simpler are almost always better.

Mass Customization

A production system that stresses the production of relatively small lots of customized or somewhat unique goods.

Comments: In manufacturing terms it is generally more profitable to produce large quantities of a single standardized product than to make small quantities of many different products. With Mass Customization however, a good many standardized techniques are used to streamline what is otherwise a difficult market to succeed in.

Mass Customization rationale might be something like; we have the equipment and personnel to anodize, machine, paint, and sand blast products so we can create alternate brand name and somewhat unique products using these processes with a somewhat standard approach.

Example: Consumers can now purchase a pair of "custom-fit" jeans on-line to suit their particular desires.

On the manufacturing side, denim has been produced in many colours and styles and often has been cut into "blanks." Depending on the size requirements a "blank" in the range of desired specifications would then be sewn to create the custom-fit jeans.

Look for more customization in every consumer product over time and expect lead-times to become shorter and shorter as suppliers compete for your money.

Mass Production

Large-scale, generally very standardized manufacturing practice with high-volume production and output.

Comments: Those companies engaged in "Mass Production" today are in serious trouble if they do not implement Lean Manufacturing techniques.

Not long ago warehouses full of inventory were considered assets. Today we recognize the waste inherent in carrying large inventories.

Example: To use an extreme example, if your company produces three types of automobiles "A", "B", and "C" and you want to "Mass Produce" for maximum efficiency then you might schedule your plant to build type "A" cars during the first 4 months of the year, type "B" cars during the second 4 months, and type "C" cars during the final 4 months of the year. This would limit costly changeovers and downtime from switching models so often.

The problem is self-evident as the Lead-Time for any particular car is 1 – 4 months if it is "in season" and up to 12 months if the season just barely ended for the type of car you want to purchase.

Flexible Lean plants can make all three types of cars anytime and during any season.

Master Schedule

Overall sequenced schedule of multiple orders through a factory.

Comments: Some poor guy may be known as the "Master Scheduler" or in many cases a software package now generates a Master Schedule. (Which everyone sort of pays attention to until it is no longer convenient or there is a "hot" order that needs prioritizing.

Materials Handling

The function of moving objects from one location to another.

Comments: In a Lean environment Materials Handling becomes a bit of a science rather than an aside to manufacturing. Lean systems require fairly exacting quantities of correct materials to feed processes very quickly and then require changing again to different materials and quantities usually on-the-fly.

When done well efficient material handling supplies work areas just before they need the new supplies to continue to operate or changeover to new products.

Of course Materials Handling also must deal with more routine palletizing and storing finished goods for shipping as well as loading trucks, operating cranes, forklifts, etc. A great crew can significantly reduce losses due to damage caused by moving items around. We have tapped into the skills of Materials handling personnel many times to streamline warehouses and put raw materials at "Point of Use" locations for easy access.

Materials Requirements Planning

Using software, Materials Requirements Planning (MRP) is accomplished through evaluating the Bill of Materials (BOM), Inventory Data, and the Master Schedule in order to stimulate replenishment of materials to be consumed and present purchase orders (Po's) for future materials needed.

Multi Functional Teams

Groups formed from people with varying skill-sets typically across departments to achieve a business goal.

Comments: Groups become "Teams" when they behave like teams. Using Multi functional Teams can be of great benefit to most companies especially when they work with complex issues that require expertise from numerous backgrounds.

With many of our Kaizen events we will create a "Kaizen Team" that includes operators form the area we are working on, staff from "feeding" and "supplying" areas, a supervisor, a maintenance tech, perhaps a secretary, and maybe even a janitor.

Although Multi functional Teams generally refers to specific expertise and skill-sets, one should never overlook the benefits of having many pairs of "fresh eyes" on a problem solving team.

Non Value Adding

Any process or event that does not make a product more like what a customer is willing to pay for.

Comments: This is a very simple definition but has far reaching implications. Lean Manufacturing is almost completely about removing waste from manufacturing and processes. Waste is best defined as "any process that does not add value to a product."

To appreciate the definition of "NVA" we should revisit the concept of "VA" or "Value-Adding" which states that "Value-Adding" activities are "Any activity that makes a product more like what a customer is willing to pay for."

No customers want to pay for activities that do not "add value" to their products. The fact is all customers indirectly pay for Non-Value-Adding activities because suppliers build them into the sales price of everything they produce.

Example: Customers want "widgets" delivered to them. A supplier company makes great widgets, but has to move them to shipping (NVA), put them in boxes (NVA), and ship them (NVA). These activities were essential, but none of them made the widgets anymore valuable to the customer.

From the standpoint of the widget supplier all of these activities constitute "COSTS" or "Operating Expenses."

Operations

A broad term suggesting administrative responsibilities and duties related to office functions, manufacturing, procurement, distribution, various management issues, and global accountability.

Comments: If a person is an "Operations Manager" they will normally take on many of the responsibilities in the above definition. They may also be directly accountable for profit and loss realizations and directing the global activities of a corporation.

Operations can also be a term to describe the day to day activities a Plant Manager must engage in to keep the plant running. Often you will see titles like; Director of Operations, Director of Manufacturing Operations, or "COO" Chief Operations Officer. Each of these titles implies significant accountability and leadership even though specific areas of accountability will differ.

It is also common to refer to various processes as "Operations." Some examples include the anodizing operation, the welding operation, the plating operation, etc.

Overall Equipment Effectiveness

Overall Equipment Effectiveness (OEE) is the Combined Measurement of Equipment Availability, Performance Rate and Quality Rate. A key measurement in "Total Productive Maintenance" (TPM)

Formula: Machine Availability X Performance Rate X Quality Rate.

Comments:

Machine Availability: Is The Actual Time Left For Production After You Subtract All Planned Downtime.

Performance Rate: Is The Measure Of "How Well The Machine Was Running When It Was Running."

Quality Rate: Tells Us How Many Good Parts VS. Defective Parts A Machine Has Produced During The Time It Was Running.

OEE is an essential measurement for determining the effectiveness of your equipment and beginning to understand where up-time improvements are possible.

Painted Floor

Coloured lines or shapes painted or taped on a floor that provide Visual Cues/Information.

Comments: Variations of this technique are used to provide a very quick reference or assessment regarding stock levels that would not require physically counting the stock.

Example: Many companies that use this tool might tape or paint a floor or wall with three basic colours to indicate the "status" of out-of-stock or in-stock items.

Painted or taped up a wall you might see:
Red: Bottom several feet of a wall to immediately communicate "if stock is down to this level we are in trouble!"

Yellow: Next several feet of a wall to visually communicate "We are sure getting close to running out of stock, make more now."

Green: Highest several feet of wall to visually communicate "Our stock level for this product is fine."

5S Visual Workplace uses a version of this tool to paint or tape walkways, locations for things such as pallets, danger zones, electrical boxes, carts, totes, etc.

Pareto Chart

A graphical tool for ranking causes of problems from most significant to least significant. It is based on the Pareto principle, first defined by Juran, 1950. Pareto Charts suggest most effects (or results), come from relatively few causes; that is, 80% of effects come from 20% of the possible causes.

Comments: Almost all companies use Pareto Charts to gain a better sense of or appreciation for data collected. As consultants we have literally seen thousands of Pareto Charts and they all kind of start to blend together after awhile.

Pareto Charts are great to use, but use them in moderation. Very often we will see entire walls dedicated to Pareto Charts that are largely or entirely ignored. Perhaps too much of a good thing.

Process

A results driven, formula based, set of activities that produces an outcome.

Alternate Definition: A series of activities that collectively accomplish a distinct objective.

Comments: In Lean Manufacturing terms a process is a recipe for how something is done. Processes are also closely scrutinized for improvement opportunities.

Example: Even making a peanut butter and jelly sandwich involves passing through a process. If all of the ingredients for your sandwich are located in your kitchen except your jelly which is located in the Garage, then you would clearly have a process improvement opportunity.

Process Map

A work flow diagram which depicts the elements of a work flow often using time, people, and machine information to illustrate tasks and results.

Comments: Process maps can be used as a starting point for beginning a Value Stream Mapping exercise to find "Value-Adding" steps in a process.

Process Re-Engineering

A discipline that uses a set of tools to analyze a company's practices and evaluate them as compared to "Best-In-Class" companies for the purpose of improving those practices.

Comments: The lines between Process Re-engineering, 6 Sigma, and Lean often become a bit fuzzy. Certainly each discipline contributes to the available tools and knowledge accessible from any of these three frameworks or approaches.

Productivity

The scaled amount of benefit realized as derived from inputs.

Comments: In Lean Manufacturing terms we are always looking for more ways to be productive which raises "productivity."

There is an old joke about a farmer selling watermelons who figured out he was losing about 8 or 10 cents per melon when it came time to sell them. He decided he would have to make it up on volume.

If you don't understand the joke we are in real trouble here! Doing the "right" things productively is always good. Building inventory to be "productive" when there are no sales or you are losing money on the products is always bad. Sometimes we see productivity numbers that brag about success while profit margins show the opposite.

We realize uses of this term vary somewhat.

Prototype

A mock-up of a product or process that is still in design mode.

Alternative definition: A prototype is an early sample or model built to test a concept or process or to act as a thing to be replicated or learned from. It is a term used in a variety of contexts, including semantics, design, electronics, and software programming.

A prototype is designed to test and trial a new design to enhance precision by system analysts and users. Prototyping serves to provide specifications for a real, working system rather than a theoretical one.

Quality Audit

A systematic and usually independent examination of a company's commitment to quality practices to verify if quality related activities are implemented effectively and comply with the company's or industries quality systems and/or quality standards.

Comments: Both "Internal" (conducted by in-house auditors) and "External" (conducted by outside/independent auditors) quality audits are common in most globally operating companies.

Quality-By-Design

The process used to design quality into products, service, or processes during the product development phase.

Comments: It is always better to "start with quality" rather than to try and "build quality in." Sure it is a bit cliché, but many companies spend most of their existence trying to make-up for poor design.

Rapid Prototyping

A process that avoids creating conventional tooling thereby limiting investment expense while new parts or products are tested for feasibility of manufacture.

Comments: This is a very exciting area for improvements in manufacturing generally. Some Rapid Prototyping software and devices are maturing to the point where it is starting to become possible in the near future that we will be telling computers to "make a basketball" or "make a fuel injection system." Pardon the reference to Star Trek, but some of the equipment we have seen begins to resemble the "Replicator" technology that sits on most countertops (much like a microwave), in the crew quarters on the Starship Enterprise.

Don't be surprised if Rapid Prototyping quickly evolves into Rapid Creation. The face of many industries will be changing significantly as this technology develops.

Single Minute Exchange of Die

Single Minute Exchange of Die (SMED) is the Lean tool used to very quickly change machines or processes over from producing a specific part number or product to producing a different part number or product or changing an attribute(s) of the current part number or product. SMED processes are highly choreographed and rehearsed to minimize machine downtime.

Comments: Generally when we speak of SMED we are talking about changing machines over by taking out dies or mechanical structures and replacing them with other dies or structures. It is also very common to change from one colour, flavour, thickness, etc. to another. Generally there is a certain amount of "purging" of current product to allow for the introduction of the "new" product or specific different elements.

Many companies now recognize the importance for minimal machine downtime during changeovers and have created entire systems for completing changeovers and setups very quickly. Likewise, many equipment manufacturers have begun integrating quick change systems into capital equipment as a major selling point.

Standardized Work

Repeating work activities using the same processes every time.

Comments: Standardized Work will generally include testing work processes again and again to prove out the "Current best ways" of completing tasks. The "current best ways" is an important concept as one of the basic tenants of Standardized Work is that you are always looking for better ways to do work.

Normally when we help companies implement Standardized Work we use photos, simple diagrams, and plain text to make work instructions and present them in a very clear manner.

It is difficult to get consistent quality and timely output unless you standardize work processes and write "Standardized Work Instructions" that must be followed. Most workers like to do things "their own way," and that is fine as long as their way is the standardized way. If workers wish to challenge the "Standardized Work Instructions" that is fine and even appreciated. The key is that everyone should be completing whatever task in the "Current Best Way."

Special Note: If ever the need for stopwatches is warranted please let your operators do the timing. Few things displease and disrespect operators more than a manager or supervisor hanging over their shoulder with a stopwatch timing their every move. Trust me on this one.

Supply Chain Management

The tool used to pass data and expectations between suppliers and customers with the primary purpose for the customers being to have what is needed, in the quantity and quality needed, and at the lowest possible price.

Comments: Managing Supply Chains has become an area of specialization in which entire careers are now built. Expectations on suppliers to lower prices, ship on-demand or forecast with increasing perfection are common. Many customers expect suppliers to replenish the stock in-house requiring visits from supplying companies on a regular basis.

As an increasing trend customers are requiring suppliers to delay billing for materials supplied until those materials have been consumed in-house or in some cases until outside customers have purchased finished goods that contain the materials from the original supplier.

Can anyone say "Cash-Flow"? Stricter requirements are pushing suppliers to limits in many cases essentially weeding-out smaller companies from the supplying base.

Systems Integration

A process whereby all elements of a product are incorporated and usually tested in order to insure proper functions per customer specifications.

Comments: This can also include installing customized components on-site in customer companies to guarantee proper "matching" and usability of the manufactured product or device.

Takt Time

Matching the rate of production to the rate of sales or consumption.

Comments: Takt Time (a German word for meter or measure) is often compared to a metronome symbolizing "keeping time." in its purest sense Takt Time is used to only produce exactly what your customers will consume; nothing more and nothing less.

In practical application knowing what Takt Time is for a specific product can help you understand the level of effort you will have to exert to meet your customer's demand.

Using an "easy math" example: If your customer wishes to buy 10 products from you every day and your normal production shift is 10 hours, then your Takt Time is 1 part per hour.

Producing only 9 parts per day would create a shortfall and leave your customer waiting. Producing 11 parts per day would create excess inventory and all the inherent problems that come with excess inventory.

Teams

Groups of people that collaborate to achieve common goals. See "Empowered Teams"

Comments: We love working with Teams, especially if they are "Empowered Teams." Two heads are definitely better than one and Teams will almost always come up with better answers and improvements than a single person can on their own.

Look for Teams to almost completely replace standard hierarchal supervisory structures and systems in the future. This seems to be the natural evolution of self-direction in manufacturing today and going forward.

Team Leader

The representative of the team for which they are a member of.

Comments: A "Team Lead" may have some supervisory responsibilities, but largely is "just one of the team" meaning they roll their sleeves up and work just like everyone else.

Generally we encourage companies using Team Systems to allow team members to "elect" their own Leads and encourage them to rotate who fills the Lead role (as well as other roles), on a periodic basis.

Team Leads can be seen as the liaison between supervision, management, other departments, etc. This structure tends to streamline communications as the Lead disseminates needed information to the rest of the team.

Throughput

The rate at which work proceeds through a manufacturing system.

Comments: Generally speaking the greatest inhibitor to Throughput is waste. Machine downtime, waiting for materials, out of stock supplies, operator errors, poorly designed processes, etc. all contribute to poor throughput in a manufacturing system.

All Lean improvements ultimately result in increased throughput of company products. In the "ideal" Lean environment materials are brought directly to the first processing area, processed as needed throughout the system, and loaded onto trucks or rail cars etc.

Increasing Throughput is always a function of eliminating waste found throughout the system. Even small improvements that eliminate or reduce waste can have a cumulative effect on overall throughput.

Tiers of Suppliers

Upstream activities are divided into tiers of suppliers

Tier 1 Supplier
(a.k.a. Prime Contractor, Prime) A supplier with prime or paramount design responsibilities for key systems, subsystems, or components as pertaining to end product(s).

Tier 2 Supplier
(a.k.a. Sub-Contractor, Sub) A supplier to Tier 1 Suppliers or a direct supplier of less critical components, systems or subsystems.

Time Based Competition

The belief that the originator or first producer/vendor of a product has a significant market advantage over other companies. See also "Time to Market"

A bi-product of this "race to market" is that competing companies must adapt their organizations in ways to minimize the time it takes to develop a product to exploit the "First on the scene" advantage.

Time to Market

The length of time it takes to develop a new product from inception until its' first market sales.

Comments: Products are being developed so quickly that companies must strike a balance between being "first on the scene" with new products and giving away under-developed ideas that competitors may improve on with lightning speed.

Consider what has happened with mobile phones in the last few years. Speed and "features" have been competing in this market and there seems to be no end in sight.

Total Quality Management

Total Quality Management (TQM) is a Quality Control System focused on the correction of quality issues before they are permitted to subsequently be passed on for further processing. TQM systems are often "built-in" to manufacturing processes.

Comments: TQM has significantly raised the awareness for the need to address quality concerns early in processing so as to limit losses of high-value parts or products.

Total Productive Maintenance

Total Productive Maintenance (TPM) is an equipment maintenance system that proactively addresses maintenance issues before they become major problems and cause equipment downtime.

Comments: TPM engages machine operators and staff in the routine maintenance of equipment so machines are constantly maintained on a basic level. More advanced maintenance procedures are still performed by skilled maintenance professionals.

TPM efforts include putting machines on a schedule so that all of their maintenance needs are addressed on a regular basis without overlooking essential steps and processes.

A good TPM program will free-up maintenance workers so they can address urgent and critical repairs that result in immediate downtime. Maintenance staff will also have additional time to allot to more proactive and preventative maintenance overall.

Operators and production staff generally wait less for maintenance dept. assistance and learn some new ways they can resolve minor machine issues without need for further maintenance support. Truly, everyone wins when a TPM program is functioning as it should.

TPM is great fun to implement and virtually always results in a dramatic reduction of wastes due to downtime immediately and in the long-run.

True Capacity

The "real attainable volume" at full utilization of a manufacturing system or subsystems after deducting for "normal events" such as machine maintenance, known bottlenecks, etc.

Comments: This is a fairly fluid concept and will change by degree for various reasons. In other words, it is more of a construct to help you have a "sense" of your real capacity, but is not any sort of exact measurement.

Value Adding

(a.k.a. VA, Value-Added, Value-Add) Any activity that makes a product more like what a customer is willing to pay for.

Comments: Lean Manufacturing is about eliminating waste which is "Non-Value-Adding" (NVA), in order to strictly and consistently focus on Value-Adding activities which customers are more than happy to pay for.

Eliminating NVA activities is easier said than done and for this reason many Lean Tools have been developed in order to achieve this end.

Variation

Any difference(s) that exist between design specifications and actual output.

Comments: Manufacturing always experiences variation by degree. In some settings "give or take a few inches" and your product is still well within tolerance and customer specs. In other settings perhaps only a few microns will make the difference between a "good part" and a piece of scrap.

Virtual Prototyping

Software-based engineering process that includes the use of modelling in multiple dimensions and in software simulated "normal operating conditions" in order to discover weaknesses, design improvement opportunities, and general refinement before physically building a tangible prototype.

Comments: Whatever the undertaking it generally pays great dividends to invest time and effort very heavily into the "front-end" of a product rather than try to "work the bugs out" after it has gone to manufacturing. Once again with "Speed to Market" concerns a balance must be struck so as to not lose out to faster competitors.

Waste

(a.k.a. "MUDA" in Japanese) Any activity which utilizes equipment, materials, parts, space, employee time or other corporate resource beyond the minimum amount required for value-added operations to insure manufacturability.

Work Cells

(a.k.a. U-Shaped Cells, Work Cells) Generally a horseshoe or U-Shaped work area layout that enables workers to easily move from one process to another in close proximity and pass parts between workers with little effort. "Cells" typically focus on the production of specific models in "part families" but can be adjusted to many different products as needed.

Comments: Work Cells do not need to be in a U-shaped configuration though this is often common due to maximizing product throughput with minimal use of space. We have created Work Cells in many different configurations that resemble letters like T, W, X, V, etc.; it is also common to create polygons, circles, rectangles, etc.

The ultimate layout of the cell is determined by the needs of the product. The goal in laying out a new Work Cell is to pass a part through every needed process with the minimal amount of wasted motion and distance. On the next level the layout of the Work Cell is determined by the manual and machine cycle times and "Takt Time" in order to determine Cell staffing.

Other issues when creating cells include redundancy of equipment; size of equipment needed, cure times, and Cell mobility/flexibility to accommodate multiple products.

When Work Cells are laid out most efficiently they can usually produce parts with a staff of 1 person moving from station to station (Load-Load) or fully staffed with a worker at each station. Product demand helps determine staffing.

Conclusion

We should conclude this book by reminding ourselves about the 5 key principles guide the Lean philosophy and approach to Continuous Improvement are built on:

Customers: Specify value from the standpoint of the customer. Understand who your customer(s) are and identify what is important to them.

Value Stream: Identify the value stream for each product or service; the value stream is the steps and activities done to deliver the product or service to the customer.

Flow: Make the steps occur so the product or service will flow smoothly toward the customer. Eliminate steps that do not create value for the customer.

Pull: As flow is introduced, pull is established by producing or servicing based on customer demand.

Continuous Improvement: Seek perfection, begin the process again and continue to make improvements and celebrate success.

Keep improving!!